30 Minutes To Ripped

Get Your Dream Body Fast with Body Weight Exercises Today!

Cathy Harwell

Cathy Harwell

Cathy Harwell

Contents

Introduction

I want to thank you and congratulate you for buying the book, "30 Minutes to Ripped – Get Your Dream Body Fast with Body Weight Exercises Today".

This book contains proven exercises that will burn fat, build muscle, and tone your body all with just the use of your own bodyweight. Calisthenics is a very popular form of exercising that when coupled with the right nutrition will rapidly transform your body. In this book you will be provided 14 exercises, a nutrition plan, and a 21-day workout regimen that will boost you to achieving your dream body faster than you can imagine.

Use these exercises and information to help turn your life around towards a healthier and more fit you!

Thanks again for buying this book, I hope you enjoy it!

Chapter 1 - What Is Calisthenics

Calisthenics is a type of exercise that is done without using any equipment, but instead it is done by using the weight of the body to build muscle. These exercises are often done in a rhythmic motion by the use of gross motor skills. The great thing about calisthenics is that you do not need to go out and buy any expensive equipment, you do not need to buy a gym membership, you do not need a trainer and do not have to purchase a bunch of complicated exercise videos.

All you have to do is use your own body to help you lose weight and build muscle. Besides not having to spend a ton of money on products that you will likely not use, when you are using your body to do calisthenics you are focusing on controlling your body instead of focusing on how much you can lift. Think about it this way. If you practice lifting you are going to become very good at lifting because we all know that practice makes perfect, but if you are practicing controlling your body that is what you will become good at.

Another benefit of using calisthenics instead of weight lifting is that unlike weight lifting calisthenics promotes the building of lean muscle mass whereas weight lifting gives you bulk. This means that calisthenics can be used by both men and women without anyone having to worry about becoming overly bulky.

Of course, there is nothing wrong with lifting weights if that is what you want to do than I fully support it, but since you are reading this book I am going to guess that lifting weights is not for you.

If you want to be stronger and leaner than calisthenics is for you, but if you are looking to bulk up the exercises that I am going to teach you in this book are not going to benefit you. On the other hand, if you want to lose weight and build lean muscle mass than you are going to love what calisthenics can do for you.

Calisthenics can be used by anyone of any fitness level. Even if you have never exercised in your life you can do calisthenics. You don't have to worry about keeping up with the girl dancing across the screen like you do when you purchase an aerobics video, you can also work at your own pace so if it takes you a little longer to do 10 reps than that is fine.

The first thing that you have to do when it comes to calisthenics is to set a goal. Let's say that you have never worked out, but you want to be able to do 100 reps of a specific exercise. You don't have to worry about doing 100 reps on your first day of working out that is your long term goal. For your short term goal, maybe you will do 5 reps of that specific exercise each day for a week. Then the next week you may decide that you can do 7 reps followed by 10 the following week and so on.

With each exercise I give you in this book, you are going to have to set a goal for yourself. In the last chapter of this book I am going to have a 21-day challenge for you that will help you work up to more reps per exercise, but if this challenge does not work for you then you can create one of your own by using this guideline.

After you have decided how many reps you want to do of each exercise you need to think about the big picture. Why are you doing calisthenics? Do you want to lose weight? How much weight do you want to lose? Do you want to build lean muscles? How strong do you want to be?

What other exercises are you going to add into your workout? You see the great thing about calisthenics is that you can do 10 reps here and 5 reps there when you have a few minutes to spare, but you also want to be getting some aerobic exercise on top of your calisthenics.

I am not going to spend much time talking about this because I want to focus on calisthenics, but if you want to lose weight you have to do more than just build lean muscle mass. Of course that is going to help you lose weight, but there is more to it than that.

You will also need to pick an aerobic exercise that you can do a few times a week that you enjoy. This is important and it goes for calisthenics too. If you do not enjoy your workout you are not going to stick to it and if you don't stick to it, you will never see results. The reason for this is because instead of enjoying what you are doing you are going to dread it every day. You are going to feel as if it is a chore that you have to do and that you do not want to do. If you don't want to do it, you are going to find reasons not to do it.

So choose an aerobic exercise that will work for you and that you will stick with. Even if you have to switch it up every few days, keep it interesting and make sure you are having fun.

Chapter 2 – Nutrition

You are never going to be healthy or lose weight if you do not change the way you are eating. Nutrition is just as important and exercise when it comes to weight loss. Your body has to have the right fuel if you want it to work properly and that is where nutrition as well as hydration come into play.

I am a huge advocate for clean eating. Personally, I believe that if food is made in a lab it should not be put into our bodies. You cannot expect that if you fill your body with a bunch of chemicals that it will function properly.

For that reason, I want to talk about processed food. Let's start with all of the processed food that is 'low fat' 'no fat' 'sugar free' and other diet foods. The truth is that the low fat and no fat or reduced fat foods still contain the same amount of sugar if not more than the original product because sugar is fat free. When it comes to sugar free foods, these are just as bad for you because instead of using sugar they are replacing it with sweet chemicals.

Now you may be thinking, oh but sugar is natural. Sugar cane is natural what you are buying at the store and what is being put into your food is refined sugar. The white flour that is used in our food has been bleached and stripped of its nutrients. Other foods such as Cheetos are nothing more than science experiments.

I could talk about how bad this food is for you all day but I won't. I just want you to understand how it affects your body. I highly suggest that you watch the movie FEDUP if you want to really understand what you are doing to your body by eating these types of food.

Some people can give these foods up cold turkey, but I suggest that you do it slowly so that you do not cause your body to go through withdrawals. The sugar that is added into these foods actually causes your brain to have a similar reaction as cocaine. It is very addictive and like cocaine it will cause your body to have symptoms if you do not feed the addiction. You may feel very sick during your first week without refined sugar, light headed and tired a well. This is all normal and is something you should prepare for.

Now that you know what you should not eat you need to learn what you should eat. Natural fruits, veggies, meat and dairy products are what you need to focus your entire diet around. Instead of fizzy drinks, make sure that you are getting enough water. You need to stay hydrated if you want your body to burn the fat off and if you want to build muscle.

Dairy products are something that needs a little more explaining than fruits, veggies and meat do. This is because people are so confused about what dairy products to eat. They drink skim milk, use vegetable oil spread and low fat cheeses thinking that they are doing their bodies a favor, but the truth is you are causing harm to your body by doing this.

You need to drink whole milk, use REAL butter and eat REAL cheese. No more American Cheese slices, these are not cheese, but cheese product and if you look up a video on YouTube showing how it is made you will never touch it again. The reason that you are eating these products is because they are as close to their natural state as possible and that is what you want to aim for.

You need to focus on eating foods that are as close to their natural state as possible. This does not mean that all of your meals have to be raw, they can be cooked but when you eat fruits and veggies it is best to eat as many raw as you can.

Of course you will not be able to go 100 percent without processed foods, but a good rule of thumb to go by is that it is okay to eat it as long as there are 3 ingredients or less and you know what those ingredients are. (I have even found chocolate bars like this)

When you are eating this way you are going to need to eat A LOT. The foods that you will be eating do not contain the amount of calories that you are used to. The great thing about taking on this lifestyle change is that you will never be hungry.

Think about this. For the number of calories, you would get in a regular sized snickers bar you can eat two and a half bananas. What is great about this is that you are not going to need to eat two and a half bananas for a snack so this means that you are going to be saving calories as well as giving your body the nutrients that it needs.

When it comes to meals you are going to have to make sure that you are getting at least 14 grams of fiber for every 1000 calories you are eating each day, 2 cups of fruit, 2.5 cups of vegetables, 46 grams of protein for women and 56 for men.

You also need to make sure you are eating enough complex carbohydrates, starchy carbohydrates and healthy fats. If you do not get these, you are going to feel drained and just sick. Avocados are a great way to get the healthy fats that you need, potatoes will provide your starchy carbohydrates and complex carbs will come from beans, whole grains, nuts, seeds and fruits and vegetables.

You should also aim to drink at least 8 glasses of water per day. Each morning when you wake up instead of going right for the coffee, grab a glass of water and squeeze the juice from one lemon into it. This will give your metabolism a boost as soon as you wake up and this will help you burn more calories throughout the day.

When you think you are hungry, drink a glass of water before you eat. Often times people confuse thirst for hunger, and this causes them to overeat. When you begin drinking the amount of water your body actually needs you will find that it is much easier to lose weight.

Chapter 3 – Exercises

Now it is time to get down to the basics of calisthenics. In this chapter I am going to go over 12 different calisthenics that you can use and I will also provide a link to a video so that you can see how the exercise is actually done.

1. **Chest dip**- This exercise is going to focus on your chest and it is one of the few exercises that will require you to have more than just your body. To do this exercise you are going to need two parallel bars. Most of the time you can find these bars at a park or a gym. Many people will tell you that this exercise should work your biceps and triceps but that is not true. This exercise should focus on the chest alone with very little work being done by the biceps and triceps. Here is a link to a video explaining how it is done.

   https://www.youtube.com/watch?v=tUOETUfcCEI

2. **Pushups**- This is one of the most basic exercises, but it is a total body exercise. Pushups are used to strengthen the upper body and they help to build the strength of the core. Pushups work several muscle groups at the same time. These include the chest, arms, triceps, neck, back and shoulders. They also promote good posture and provide stability to the torso. Pushups also build muscle endurance and promote overall fitness this is why military personnel use pushups as part of their exercise regimen. Pushups are very easy to do and there are several different types of pushups which target different groups of muscles. This video will show

you how to do a basic pushup for beginners and several variations as well.

https://www.youtube.com/watch?v=NECcLiefyoM

3. **Squats**- This exercise is going to work the entire leg and even some parts of your lower back. This is an all in one exercise for the legs and you can literally feel every part of your legs being engaged. Here is a link to a great video showing you how you can do squats properly.

https://www.youtube.com/watch?v=rXJzj9K3sxU

4. **Lunges**- This exercise also engages the lower body and is a great work out for the thighs. Lunges also work the hip muscles, the lower leg muscles and the abdominal muscles. It is a great exercise to help build your core and help you focus on posture as well. Here is a great video that will help you learn how to do a proper lunge.

https://www.youtube.com/watch?v=vNgs9aguMw4

5. **Crunches**- This exercise will help you to build your core by working your abdominal muscles. It will also help you focus on controlling your body because it is important that you control each of your movements while you are doing crunches. Here is a simple video that shows exactly how this is done.

https://www.youtube.com/watch?v=73CmRbQKDjY

6. **Bench dips**- This exercise is used for working your triceps. This is the area on the top back of your arm. Women often struggle with this area of their arms accumulating fat, but by using this exercise you can burn that fat and build lean muscle mass. Here is a video that explains how it is done.

https://www.youtube.com/watch?v=dl8_opVoAoY

7. **Scissor kicks**-This exercise is great for working the muscles that are deep inside your hips, but it will also help with the legs and abdominals. It is a simple exercise and is very popular because of this. Follow this link to find a video explaining how to do this exercise.

https://www.youtube.com/watch?v=nWKTmFv76I8

8. **Burpees**- This exercise is a bit more difficult than the others that we have learned this far. This is because the Burpee is a whole body movement that works every muscle group in the body. It is also known as the squat thrust and it is said that it was developed by a man named Burpee who lived in a prison where there was no workout equipment. Here is a video explaining how it is done.

https://www.youtube.com/watch?v=B3pfaQ2sDPA

9. **Knee High**- The knee high will focus on your lower abdominals much more than crunches do. When you raise your knee you are fighting against gravity, engaging your lower abdominal muscles and with each rep you will feel more and more burning in those muscles. Here is an awesome video to teach you how to do these properly.

https://www.youtube.com/watch?v=bZUfaLxJ36M

10. **Forearm plank**- This exercise will help to strengthen all of the muscles on the front of your

body, including your legs, arms, lower back, glutes and core and it has been proven to promote a positive mood. Many people believe that this looks like a very simple exercise but when you are doing it you will find that all of your muscles are engaged and it is not as easy as it looks. Here is a link to a video teaching you how to perform this exercise properly.

https://www.youtube.com/watch?v=xFGXIMoArw4

11. **Calf raises**- This exercise focuses specifically on the calf, but it will help to strengthen the knee and ankle as well. This is a very simple exercise and one that many people enjoy because it gives them that sexy calf with little effort. Here is a link to a video explaining how to do this exercise.

https://www.youtube.com/watch?v=-M4-G8p8fmc

12. **Side torso raise**- This exercise is going to help build muscle as well as work the obliges and lower body as well. You will be engaging all of your body when you are doing this exercise. Here is a video to help you learn how to do this exercise.

https://www.youtube.com/watch?v=eRu1OIm431g

Those are 12 great exercises that you can start off with and then you can add more to your routine as you become better and fit. Now that we have learned about these exercises, what muscle groups they work and hopefully you have watched all of the videos to ensure that you are doing the exercise with proper form we can move on the 21-day challenge.

Chapter 4 - 21 Day Challenge

Now that you know all about calisthenics, nutrition and the exercises that you will be preforming it is time for you to prepare for your 21 day calisthenics challenge. In this chapter, we are going to go over each day in the next 21 days detailing what exercises you should do as well as how many reps of each exercise you should do.

During this time, you will find that you are getting better and better at these exercises and that you are feeling better than you ever have in your life. On top of that you are going to be losing weight and that is what it is all about!

Remember, you are also going to be focusing on eating healthy and getting enough water every single day. If you neglect to do this, your results will suffer and you will likely get discouraged. Remember this is only 3 weeks out of your life and the benefits are worth the amount of effort you are going to have to put into it.

Day 1-

- Cardio: 20 minutes of walking

- Interval-

    o 5 pushups

    o 15 crunches

    o 10 squats

Repeat three times. When you are first starting out you can take as long as you need to take. If you are at an intermediate level, each interval should take 2 minutes and if you are advanced you should do one interval in 60 seconds.

Day 2-

- Cardio: Today your cardio is going to be a bit different. During the time that you are doing your cardio make sure that you are not taking breaks. For your cardio you will do:

  Jumping jacks for 10 seconds, knee highs for 20 seconds, jumping jacks for 30 seconds, knee highs for 40 seconds, jumping jacks for 50 seconds, knee highs for 60 seconds, jumping jacks for 50 seconds, knee highs for 40 seconds, jumping jacks for 30 seconds, knee highs for 20 seconds and finally jumping jacks for 10 seconds.

  This is only 6 minutes of exercise so stick with it and you will be able to finish.

- Interval-

  o 30 seconds of forearm plank

  o 5 burpees

Do this three times during the day.

Day 3-

- Cardio: 60 minutes of walking

- Interval-

  o 5 chest dips

  o 5 pushups

  o 3 squats

You will do this interval 5 times. If you are a beginner, you can take as long as you need. Intermediate should take no more than 2 minutes and advanced should take no more than 1 minute per interval.

Day 4-

- Cardio: 15 minutes jogging
- Interval 1-
  - 16 jumping jacks
  - 6 crunches
  - 5 side torso raises
- Interval 2-
  - 14 jumping jacks
  - 4 crunches
  - 6 side torso raises
- Interval 3-
  - 12 jumping jacks
  - 6 crunches
  - 7 side torso raises
- Interval 4-
  - 10 jumping jacks
  - 4 crunches
  - 8 side torso raises

- Interval 5-
    - 8 jumping jacks
    - 6 crunches
    - 9 side torso raises

Day 5-

- Cardio- Walk for 20 minutes
- Interval-
    - 10 squats
    - 10 pushups
    - 10 burpees
    - 10 lunges

        Repeat interval 3 times

Day 6-

- Cardio- Jog for 30 minutes
- Interval-
    - 5 burpees
    - 5 crunches
    - 5 scissor kicks
    - 5 lunges

        Repeat interval 5 times

Day 7-

- Cardio- Walk for 60 minutes
- Interval-
    - Knee highs for 60 seconds
    - 5 pushups
    - 10 lunges
    - 12 crunches
    - 12 squats
    - 12 scissor kicks

Day 8-

- Cardio- walk 20 minutes, jog 10 minutes, run 5 minutes
- Interval-
    - 10 second sprints
    - 4 pushups
    - 4 squats
    - 20 second sprints
    - 4 pushups
    - 6 squats
    - 30 second sprints
    - 8 pushups
    - 10 squats

- o   20 second sprints

- o   4 pushups

- o   6 squats

- o   10 second sprints

- o   2 pushups

- o   4 squats

Day 9-

- Cardio- 30-minute walk

- No interval

Day 10-

- Cardio- 30-minute jog followed by 30 second sprints then walk for 30 seconds. Repeat sprints 5 times.

- Interval-

  - o   12 crunches

  - o   14 squats

  - o   4 pushups

  - o   10 crunches

  - o   16 squats

  - o   6 pushups

  - o   8 crunches

  - o   14 squats

- o 4 pushups

- o 6 crunches

- o 16 squats

- o 6 pushups

Day 11-

- Cardio- 30 minutes of jogging

- Interval-

    - o 60 second forearm plank

    - o 10 side torso raises

    - o 60 second forearm plank

    - o 10 side torso raises

Day 12-

- Cardio- walk 1 mile

- Interval-

    - o 10 jumping jacks

    - o 10 pushups

    - o 10 burpees

    Rest 10 seconds and repeat interval 5 times.

Day 13-

- Cardio- Walk 1 mile with 2 pounds of extra weight.

- Interval-

- o   6 lunges

- o   8 squats

- o   6 pushups

  Repeat interval 4 times

Day 14-
- Cardio- Run 1 mile
- Interval-
  - o   10 pushups
  - o   20 crunches

    Repeat interval 4 times

Day 15-
- Cardio- Jog 2 miles
- Interval-
  - o   12 crunches
  - o   6 pushups
  - o   6 burpees
  - o   10 calf raises
  - o   Repeat 4 times

Day 16-
- Cardio- Jog 1 mile
- Interval- no interval

Day 17-
- Interval-
  - 6 squats
  - 6 crunches
  - 4 pushups
  - 6 burpees

  Repeat interval 5 times

Day 18-
- Cardio- Walk 1 mile
- 15 jumping jacks
- 15 push ups
- 15 lunges
- 10 burpees
- 15 chest dips
- 15 scissor kicks
- 15 knee highs
- 15 side torso raises
- 60 second fore arm plank

Day 19-
- Cardio- Run for 2 miles
- Interval-

- o 15 jumping jacks
- o 15 pushups
- o 15 lunges

  Repeat interval 3 times

Day 20-

- Cardio- Jog for 2 miles
- Interval-
  - o 15 lunges
  - o 15 crunches
  - o 15 calf raises
  - o 15 scissor kicks

    Repeat interval 4 times

Day 21-

- Cardio- 1-hour running
- Interval-
  - o 16 scissor kicks
  - o 6 pushups
  - o 12 lunges

    Repeat interval 5 times

That is, your 21 day calisthenics workout challenge. When you have made it this far you will look back with pride. On day 21 you are going to be a completely different person than you were on day one and that is something you can be proud of.

When you are exercising make sure that you are drinking enough water. When it is hot outside you need to be even more aware of the amount of water that you are drinking. On days when the weather does not allow you to get outside it is okay for you to substitute a different cardio exercise as long as it is done for the same amount of time that is required for that day.

As you can see there are no days off when it comes to this 21-day challenge, but that does not mean that you should not take any days off at all. If you are a beginner, I would suggest you adding in 8 days into this challenge so that your body will be able to rest. On those days you will not do any cardio and no intervals. You will instead simply allow your body to rest and recover.

Your muscles are going to get sore and there are going to be days when you absolutely do not want to do your challenge, but stick to it and you are going to see some amazing results.

Chapter 5 – Tips

To finish up this book I want to give you some tips and tricks that you can use to help you be successful with the 21-day challenge that I have given you, with changing the way you are eating and with losing those extra pounds.

The first thing that I want to talk about is that you should not change the way that you eat and take on the challenge at the same time. Remember when I told you earlier in the book that when you remove the processed foods from your diet that you will feel sick? You do not want to be going through this while you are trying to take on the challenge because one of the two changes if not both are going to fail.

Instead, you should change the way you eat, focusing on removing the processed foods from your diet for the first 30 days. Once you have a handle on what is going into your body you can focus on the 21-day challenge. There is no faster way for you to lose the weight and keep it off than doing the things that you have learned in this book and I encourage you to give it a try.

The second tip that I have for you is to create a new routine. You are going to have to set a specific time each day to do all of your cardio. You also need to schedule a specific time each day to do your intervals as well. If you just say that you will get to it at some point in your day, it will not happen. To promote your own success you need to have a plan.

If you are just starting out, you can break your intervals up throughout the day. For example, if an interval were to say 5 pushups, 5 lunges, 5 burpees- repeat 5 times, you can do this at 5 separate times during the day. This will help you from feeling overwhelmed and it will help to ensure that you do not develop muscle soreness early on which could cause you to give up.

If your muscles do get sore soaking in a hot tub with a cup of Epsom salt will help to relax them. You can also eat extra bananas and extra protein to help control muscle soreness. Water is also one of the best things you can use to help prevent muscle soreness. I cannot say it enough; you need to make sure that you are drinking enough water.

Make sure that you are getting enough sleep when you are going through this challenge. Getting enough sleep is important all of the time, but even more so when you are going through huge lifestyle changes you may find that you need even more sleep. You want to aim for 8-9 hours of sleep per night when you are going through the 21-day challenge so that you are not exhausting your body.

Make sure that you are consistent with your workout routine. If your workout only one or two days a week you are not going to see results. If you want to be successful in this challenge you need to stick with it and do everything that is needed for the duration of the challenge. Once the challenge is over do not feel as if you can quit exercising and go back to your old lifestyle. You have to make the choice to make a lifestyle change because if you do go back to your old lifestyle you will only gain the weight that you lost back and you will lose the muscle that you gained. This is not an easy challenge and even though it is worth putting the work in, it is not worth it if you are just going to go back to your old lifestyle.

Make sure that you are setting realistic goals when it comes to any exercise routine. I am not going to lie to you and tell you that this 21-day challenge is going to make you lose 50 pounds in a month. What I will tell you is that it is going to help you lose weight in a healthy manner and keep it off. You should set your goal for about 2 pounds of weight loss per week. Any more than that can be unhealthy. Of course the amount of weight that you will lose will depend on the amount of weight that you have to lose. I have seen people lose as much as 10 pounds in a week and for them that was fine because they had a large amount of weight to lose. If you do experience that type of weight loss, it is important for you to understand that eventually it will slow down.

You should also use the buddy system when it comes to this challenge. When we use a buddy system for losing weight, we have someone to hold us accountable. When we don't feel like exercising we have someone to help motivate us. When we feel like we want to eat an entire carton of ice cream you have someone to talk you out of it. And when you feel discourage you have someone who is going to be by your side and talk to you about how you are feeling. The best part is that they have probably been through the same problems and you have probably helped them.

Those are the tips that I have for you. I hope that you have a lot of success with the information that I have given you in this book. Everything that you have learned will help you reach your goal of weight loss if you stick to the plan that I have given you.

Conclusion

Calisthenics is gaining popularity very quickly and becoming one of the best ways to gain a strong, lean, and toned body. The best part is that you don't even need a gym membership as everything can be done with just your bodyweight. In addition to gaining muscle calisthenics is also better on your joints than weight training because your joints aren't straining to hold up unnaturally heavy objects. Not only that but many of the exercises can be done anywhere which ends up saving you loads of time!

I hope this book will enable you achieve your dream body and weight loss goals that you desire.

Thank you again for buying this book and please leave a review on amazon!

Related Reading

I have the perfect complement to this book on calisthenics to further help you with your fitness and weight loss goals. In order to maximize the effects of your calisthenics workout you need to fully understand how your diet can have a huge impact on the effectiveness of your workout. Just making a few simple tweaks to your current eating patterns can quickly produce visible results.

I highly recommend you check out the book, ***Ketogenic Diet – Amazing 30 Day Weight Loss Plan. Start Your Anti-inflammatory Diet Today!***'. It is available on Amazon in digital format.

Cathy Harwell

<u>Scan the Above Code or Go Here to View on Amazon:</u>

http://www.amazon.com/dp/B0124PD6LS/

Stop... Before you close this book get your free bonus...

Scan Above to Claim Bonus

Or Go To: http://bit.ly/1NKyFuQ

101 Life Success Tips – Start Accomplishing Your Goals Today!
Steve Williams is a motivational expert that has helped thousands of people accomplish their dreams and goals. Here are a few tips that he has learned along the way to improving success in his life quickly.

----

1. **Use Visualization.** Visualize what your life will be like when you accomplish your goals. If you cannot see yourself accomplishing your goals than chances are that you will not accomplish them. Remember that you are to keep your eye on the prize at the end of the road. There will be times when you feel as if you are stuck and that you are not making any progress toward your goal, but what you need to do when this happens is to remember what your life

will be like in 6 months or a year if you continue to work toward your goals. Spend a few minutes with your eyes closed visualizing how great you will feel and all of the changes that will take place in your life once you reach these goals.

2. **Read Books, a Lot of Books.** For each of these tips there is a book out there that will give you deeper insight into each tip. Spend time reading each and every day. This will not only exercise your brain as well as help you learn, but it will help to relieve the stress that you have to deal with on a day to day basis. Even if you are not reading a book about self-improvement make sure you take some time each day to read. Reading fiction books helps to release the creativity we have within ourselves, which can help you solve problems down the road.

3. **Accept That You Are Responsible for Your Life.** You are in charge of your life and no one else. You cannot blame your failures on your parents or on what happened to you when you were in high school. You need to work through any issues that you may have but while doing so understand that no one makes your life what it is except you. If you are not succeeding in life, no one has caused this except for you and when you are successful you will have no one to thank for it except yourself.

4. **Learn How to Accept Failure and LEARN from it**. Failure, it is something that all of us will face at one point in our lives no matter what we do to avoid it. You have two choices when it comes to failure, you can either allow the failure to upset you and stop you in your tracks or you can learn from the failure and change what you do in the future. One example of this may be that you are trying to

lose weight, you are tempted by a chocolate cake and end up eating all of it. Now you have failed, you can either choose to give up on your weight loss goals and eat lots of chocolate cake in the following days, which will most likely cause you to gain more weight or you can learn from your mistake, understand that you lack the will power to stop eating after a small piece of chocolate cake, avoid it in the future and move on with your diet and weight loss plan.

5. **Do the Things That You Dread the Most First.** No matter what it is that you want to do, you should always do the things that you dread the most first, this is called eating the frog. This way you are not putting these tasks off while finishing up more enjoyable tasks, you simply do them, get them out of the way and then you can move on to the tasks that you will enjoy more.

This is a brand new report that will show you 101 quick ways to improve your life success. These are just a sample. You can have the entire report <u>for free here.</u>

Cathy Harwell

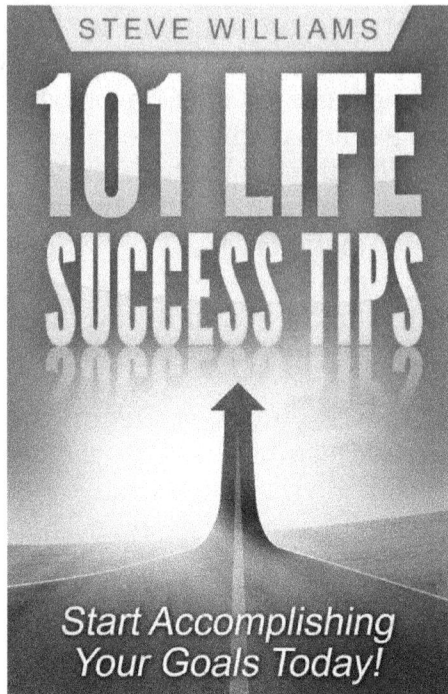

STEVE WILLIAMS
101 LIFE
SUCCESS TIPS
Start Accomplishing Your Goals Today!

Check Out My Other Books

Below, you'll find some of my other popular books on Amazon and Kindle. Simply scan the link below to visit my author page on Amazon to see my works.

Direct Link - http://www.amazon.com/Cathy-Harwell/e/B0125AD4G4/

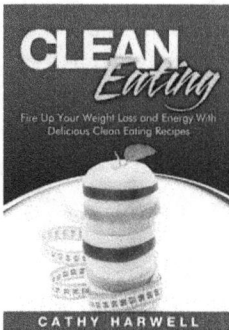

Clean Eating – Fire Up Your Weight Loss and Energy With Delicious Clean Eating Recipes

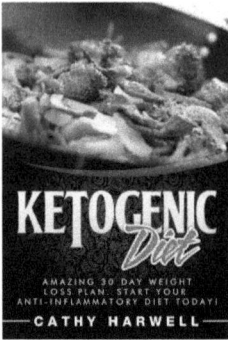

<u>Ketogenic Diet – Amazing 30 Day Weight Loss Plan Start Your Anti-Inflammatory Diet Today!</u>

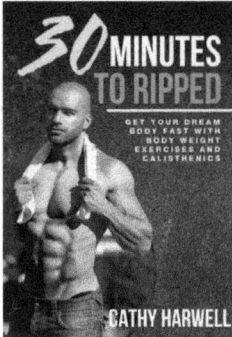

<u>30 Minutes To Ripped – Get Your Dream Body Fast With Body Weight Exercises And Calisthenics</u>

If the links do not work, for whatever reason, you can simply search for these titles on the Amazon website to find them.

www.ingramcontent.com/pod-product-compliance
Lightning Source LLC
Chambersburg PA
CBHW060950050426
42337CB00052B/3399